Timeless Commandments
for Entrepreneurial
Success

RICK MCCULLOCH

Merrimack Media ● Cambridge, MA

Library of Congress Control Number: 2014950944

ISBN: print: 978-1-939166-55-5
ISBN: ebook: 978-1-939166-56-2

This book was printed in the United States of America

Published by Merrimack Media, Cambridge, Massachusetts
September, 2014

I would like to dedicate this book to Harry Bushby who was a close cousin and long time friend who enriched the lives of everyone he touched.

Testimonials

"Rick has been very helpful in "pointing me and my business" in the right direction to accelerate growth within my company. I am extremely grateful for his guidance as well as his expertise in business development."
–Bonnie Armstrong, Mobile Marketing Allies

"Rick's seasoned mantras are bound to consolidate all your stray thoughts and incoherent wishes into a roadmap for your dreams to come true. His vast years of experience in dealing with complex situations can provide you the ease and comfort in your journey towards a successful entrepreneurship."
–Satyendra Sinha, Entrepreneur

"I had the pleasure of meeting Rick through business. Rick is a highly intelligent professional who presents his discussions and explanations based on experience and well rounded research."
–Ryu Tokumine, Entrepreneur

"Rick is a very honest and sincere Person. He has gone through tremendous efforts on himself to help guide you to where you want to go in life both personally and professionally."
–Wes Anderson, World Financial Group

"Rick McCulloch is a dedicated service-oriented delivery individual with a passion for mentoring and impacting knowledge and business development skills in the lives of those he comes across. He is honest, loyal, friendly and pragmatic and is one who goes the extra mile to get a project done even when the reward is not imminent. I found my time networking with Rick very rewarding and will recommend his book any time any day. "
–Olubiyi Ishola, MSc, P.Geo.

Contents

Foreword

You can have everything in life
you want, if you will just help
enough other people get what
they want.
—Zig Ziglar

There is no one sure path to entrepreneurial success, but there are many detours and obstacles that will inevitably arise along the journey. Anticipating and dealing with these roadblocks can mean all the difference between a life of calm and happiness versus one of frantic activity and frustration. Based on hard-won wisdom "in the arena," to use Teddy Roosevelt's metaphor, Rick McCulloch has given us a practical and insightful book that will stand the test of time. Free of the usual clichés such as "avoid procrastination," "research your market," and "believe in yourself," McCulloch gets to the heart of the key requirements for the entrepreneur. He amply demonstrates that entrepreneurs must know their own mind as well as the minds of their customers. Other books will teach you 1000 ways to research your customer and how to take advantage of the latest online fad, but few focus on timeless principles grounded in decades of experience.

Age has its privileges. The type of wisdom and insight McCulloch provides is hard to come by in our fast-paced world of instantaneous expectations and "I want it all now." McCulloch is a master synthesizer, someone who has read and studied widely while actually "doing" the work. His book reminds me of Steven Covey's The 7 Habits of Highly Effective People, which focuses on the need for character development rather than the latest gimmick for success. He has "sharpened the saw," which is a lot more than you can say about many of the success gurus who claim that they provide the "only guide" to getting ahead. You can't wish your way to success through affirmations, no matter how many times you repeat them in front of a mirror. And thinking positively is not a strategy, despite the fact that thinking negatively will get you nowhere.

In addition to providing the reader with timeless success tools and tactics, McCulloch offers up-to-date shortcuts that can save the reader from wasting valuable time and money. For example, there are free ways to streamline and automate your business, but you have to know where to find them. Analyzing your competition has never been easier, and there are tools and websites you should know about. And there is a copywriting shortcut that allows you to read the pulse of the market with a few simple steps. None of these existed a few years ago, and there is no guarantee that they won't become yesterday's news. (Does anyone really use MySpace anymore?)

Along with timeless commandments, you will find many secrets you can use today in this book. Enjoy the entrepreneurial journey, and use the roadmap that McCulloch provides as you venture forth. No matter what entrepreneurial stage you are in, you will find something of help in this book.

David Shiang

Acknowledgments

Thanks to those who inspired me: my coach, David Shiang; training seminars by JT Foxx, Michael Ervin, Les Evans, Meir Ezra; sales trainers Brian Tracy and Jeffrey Gitomer; and colleagues such as Robert Norris.

Introduction

Never, never, never give in.
–WINSTON CHURCHILL

You've seen the statistics: 50% of all new businesses in North America are out of business by the end of three years, and 95% of them fail within 10 years. Yet the lure of being your own boss has never been greater, and today it is easier to start a business than at in any time in history. As a result, more and more people are venturing out on their own. A lot of people become entrepreneurs by the desire for freedom and control. They love the idea of being their own boss and calling the shots. They want to be in control of their lives and make their own rules. They want to live life on their terms, not someone else's.

The failure rate of entrepreneurs is abysmal, with very few achieving the success they desire. But with the right mindset and actions, you can go from where you are to where you want to be. You can navigate the treacherous obstacles that lie in your path and reach your dreams.

My aim is to help you beat the odds. I will help you thrive, not just survive.

Why I Wrote this Book

There are thousands of books on entrepreneurship, small business, and achieving success. Some such as **The Autobiography of Benjamin Franklin, How to Win Friends and Influence People,** or **Think and Grow Rich** are timeless classics, whereas others teach the latest Google and Facebook tricks. Some focus on developing the success mindset; others teach negotiation, sales, marketing, and strategy. With all that has been written, you might be wondering, why another book? Didn't Ecclesiastes write in the **Bible** that "there is nothing new under the sun"? That was more than two thousand years ago. What can be said that hasn't already been said?

The answer is that I have yet to find a short, compact, and easy to read book that combines entrepreneurial shortcuts, tools, and techniques with an honest look at what is required for success. Far too many books, courses, and business programs make it appear that you can follow specific steps along a well-defined path and your success will be guaranteed. They make it seem like the entrepreneur's journey is laid out before you and all you have to do is "paint by numbers" or "follow the yellow brick road." (If you believe that, I've got a bridge to sell you.) They leave out the hard reality that the road to success is inevitably filled with obstacles, bumps, and detours. And you can't anticipate what they are going to be. Bad weather, strikes, economic upheavals, health issues, family emergencies are par for the course, not the exception.

"Expect the unexpected" might be a way of putting it, although knowing that you can't know what will happen is just the beginning. Living with uncertainty is a given in today's world, where you are expected to accomplish more with fewer resources. Astronomers tell us that the universe is expanding at an accelerated rate, and I think the same can be said for the business landscape. But although there are always more things to keep track of, you are expected to do so with fewer resources. "Do More with Less" is a constant refrain, and you need to be nimble, adaptable, and resourceful.

If you are carrying too much weight around (and it could be mental baggage that is holding you back), you aren't going to move very fast. You're going to be left wondering what happened as others who are more nimble pass you by. And if you're not focused with a sense of purpose, you're going to get waylaid by the next new thing or fad. There's nothing wrong with experimentation, but everything has its place. You need to be committed to what you are doing while being open to new approaches.

We're going to look at ways to help keep you on target so that you can make rapid progress.

It's a Jungle Out There

This book will show you how you can succeed in today's constantly-changing business environment. One of the first things you need to know about being an entrepreneur is that there is a lot of contradictory advice out there. Some people will tell you to start your company while you have a job elsewhere, others will say that you have to cut your ties so that you are fully committed. Some people will say that you should line up financing and give up equity before you start, others will tell you that you should retain control and ownership until you have proven yourself in the market so that you get a higher valuation. Some tell you to never look at email when you get up, others swear by it. There is no one size fits all and you have to find your own rhythm and cycles. But there are timeless principles that if followed, will put the odds in your favor. As Jay Abraham says, "human nature is immutable."

(And if you don't know who Abraham is, you should find out.) You need to be a student of human nature and what makes people tick if you are going to be a successful entrepreneur. Unless you own a printing press that churns out money, the material things you desire will come *through* other people. Don't even think of trying to do it alone.

Who This Book Is For

This book is for anyone who is looking for ways to accelerate their success without having to wade through thousands of pages of nice but not-very-relevant material. As they say, "nice to have" vs. "must have." My aim is to give you "must have" content, especially timeless principles about motivation and marketing. When you want more specialized knowledge on various topics, I'll give you some suggestions in my chapter on Shortcuts and Resources.

If any of the following apply to you at all, you are in the right place.

- You want a handy reference that combines timeless wisdom with current thinking that will help you succeed and reach your goals
- You know that you need to work on your mental game in order to overcome obstacles that are holding you back
- You have limited resources of time, energy, and money, and you want to discover how to maximize your effectiveness at every step of the way
- You know you have what it takes and that you can beat the odds
- You know that success is found along the journey, not upon reaching your destination. You know that waiting for

external events to materialize before you feel good is a trap. You can't say, "I will be happy when ..."

- You know that you can't do it alone

Who Am I?

Let me introduce myself. I am Rick McCulloch, an entrepreneur and small business consultant with more than 25 years of experience helping companies succeed. My specialty is the oil and gas industry, but the tools required for entrepreneurial success are basically the same no matter what industry you are in. Unlike a lot of academics who write books but have never run a business, I've been in the trenches for decades growing companies of all types. I've seen up close and personal what makes people succeed and what makes them fail.

One of my skills is identifying shortcuts, tips, and techniques that help entrepreneurs succeed. I spend a lot of time learning, and I want to give you the benefit of what I have found. I help people connect the dots so that they can expedite their progress. I've seen many people knock their heads against the wall because they aren't up-to-date on the shortcuts and secrets that can shave precious time off the things they are doing. Or they waste tons of money because they don't know simple techniques that will yield better results. Speed counts more than ever in this ever-shrinking 7 x 24 x 365 world we live in. If you aren't feeding your mind every day with ways to gain an edge (knowing full well that much of what you are going to find isn't particularly helpful), you are going to be left behind. Plain and simple.

One of my jobs is to separate the wheat from the chaff and shorten your learning curve. You can cut to the front of the line with what I am about to share with you.

1. How to Accelerate Your Success

*Try not to become a man of
success, but rather try to become
a man of value.*
–Albert Einstein

You can avoid the dismal fate of most small businesses. But you won't find a foolproof plan anywhere, despite what a lot of people will tell you. (Do you know why nothing is foolproof? Because fools are so ingenious.)

In order to succeed in today's world of entrepreneurship, far more is required than capital, teamwork, planning, and a product or service that fits the market. There are thousands of examples of companies that had all the money and talent in the world but went down the drain nevertheless. Speed to market, acting with a sense of urgency, understanding what it takes to acquire a customer, and understanding the motivations of your customers are all key.

The psychological aspects of business are often far more important than having a good product or service. Ralph Waldo Emerson said that "if you build a better mousetrap, the world will beat a path to your door," but he lived in a completely different era. Whether or not such a viewpoint was true then is not important, but it is certainly not true now. Our era is characterized by noise, clutter, and confusion, and lots of it. When AOL gave everyone 10 MB of storage in the early days, the Internet quickly became flooded with minute trivia, useless information, and downright stupidity. And it's only gotten worse. Today, low quality is drowning out high quality, and you need to find a way to rise above it all in order to get noticed.

And don't forget that IBM used to tell its sales force to instill Fear, Uncertainty, and Doubt (FUD) in the prospect's mind. You couldn't go wrong buying IBM, but if you bought from the other company, you could lose your job. The FUD Factor is alive and well when so much information is generated every day that one can't possibly keep up. Knowing what is valuable and what is not is a full-time job. (Mick Jagger used the term "useless information" in the hit song *Satisfaction*.) You need a reliable filter to help you sort things out.

Timeless Success Principles

In my extensive experience, there are a number of timeless principles that all entrepreneurs should know and practice. They have nothing to do with gaming Google or figuring out the latest Twitter trick. And while others may offer timeless thoughts too that have great value, mine go far beyond the typical suggestions about setting goals, being persistent, fostering innovation, and working with the end in mind. While the above character traits are necessary, they are hardly going to prepare you for the rough and tumble world in which you will find yourself. The principles that I am going to explore will provide you with a roadmap, a foundation, of what to expect as you go through your entrepreneurial journey. When things seem to be going haywire, take heart in the fact that you are not alone. Many have been there before you, and they have not only survived, they have thrived.

Here are some timeless principles at work in business and in life. Not all apply equally at all times, but they are filled with insight and wisdom. Some of you may not agree with me, and that's fine. There will always be exceptions. But try them on and see how well they fit before you decide that they are not for you. We'll be coming back to them in various ways, and you need to keep them in mind as you go about your everyday life. They are not in a particular order of importance, and they should be taken together and absorbed over time. I've heard about some of them for decades, and at times they take on new meaning. They can be very powerful if you use them accordingly.

Principle 1. You need to know yourself. Focus on your strengths. Outsource your limitations.

Everyone is different, and everyone has different capabilities. A management expert named Meir Ezra, who has built several million-dollar companies, estimates that the average entrepreneur possesses about 5% of the expertise and experience really required to grow a company. That's not a big number and it exposes shortcomings that most of us have. A software developer has a great idea for a product but knows very little about accounting, marketing, and legal affairs. A caterer knows a lot about cooking and the culinary arts but little about finding customers and scheduling jobs efficiently. It is no wonder that so many businesses fail to make it to the end of their 3rd year.

One of the first tasks of an entrepreneur is to take stock of his or her strengths and not try to do everything. Lower level tasks and ones that the entrepreneur doesn't want to tackle should be outsourced, using a broad definition of the word. Not everyone is good at organizing, completing things, making sales calls, and the like. You need to focus on what you do best and perfect that, not try to be a jack of all trades. You can't be all things to all people, so don't try to be that to yourself.

Apple Computer was founded by two people named Steve. Do you know the last names of both of them? Steve Jobs has become a household name for a variety of reasons. He was the showman, out front rallying the troops, persuading people to buy, and acting as his own PR and advertising firm. The technical genius behind Apple was a fellow named Steve Wozniak, and he was responsible for making sure that the products conformed to the elegant designs that Apple is famous for. Known as a technical prodigy while at Hewlett-Packard, the Woz quit his job there to found Apple. One story he tells has to do with Jobs' desire to make a small number of transistors do the work of many. In the 70's, economy of design was not much of a concern in the computer industry, and engineers simply increased processing power by adding more components. Jobs wanted everything to fit into a small space, so he challenged Wozniak to create a new design that would make fewer components do the work of many. Wozniak was initially very skeptical, but he eventually found a solution. This attitude of "doing more with less" became a standard at Apple. For Jobs, who was known as a fierce taskmaster, elegant design and robust functionality went hand in hand. He wouldn't tolerate the bulky and cumbersome phones that other manufacturers brought to the market. By insisting on "the impossible," he wound up transforming an industry as well as how consumers thought about the devices they owned. (I've heard about a wedding toast where the best man counsels the groom to hold his new bride's hand with the same love and devotion he shows his phone.)

Principle 2. People trust a perceived expert or authority. You need to rise above the crowd.

In a world where we need to make quick judgments, the ability to check someone's credentials is limited. We need to make snap judgments. If we need an emergency room doctor in a hurry, we don't interview potential candidates and asked them where they went to school, how many operations they have performed, how long they have been working, or anything of the sort. We assume that the hospital we visit employs competent physicians. Our default pattern is to defer to and believe in perceived experts and authorities. We trust that they know what they are doing. There simply isn't enough time for thorough due diligence unless the stakes are high or time is plentiful.

Note that I did not say "actual" experts and authorities, I said "perceived." For many of us, perception is reality. We view a person a certain way, and we don't have the time to dig deeper and engage in a background check that would confirm or disprove our viewpoint. We are willing to give someone the benefit of the doubt. Do you remember the movie **Catch Me If You Can**? Leonard DiCaprio played a real person named Frank Abagnale who was pursued by an FBI Agent played by Tom Hanks. In actual life, Abagnale was a check forger, thief, impostor, and counterfeiter. He was a liar and a cheat of world-class proportions. Abagnale posed as a doctor, lawyer, and airline pilot. He was able to command authority and respect, almost on call. He made people believe in him partly by dressing in the required attire and by speaking the language of the profession. He fooled a lot of people a lot of the time. (Abagnale was eventually caught, and he now works as a security consultant.)

I mention this movie because Abagnale was a master at the use of authority. Although in his case the authority was entirely fake, he knew that we respect certain professions almost automatically out of habit. We give credence to what someone says because of their uniform, their language, or their position. As consumers, we are taught to defer to experts who appear on television, radio, and in the news. If someone looks the part, we tend to believe them.

Medical doctors on television are often portrayed as sources of wisdom, and we tend to trust the doctors in our midst. Dr. Phil may not be the world's most qualified psychologist, but he is on TV and commands a huge audience. If you are just one among the hordes of ordinary people, it is much harder to command respect and be seen as having premium value. As a result, you need to stand out as well as stand above the crowd. You need to be perceived as not just different but also having a higher stature. And you need to be different in a way that matters to your target market.

Robert Cialdini, author of **Influence: the Psychology of Persuasion,** discusses six principles of influence, two of which are Authority and Social Proof. There isn't time here to go through all six principles in detail, but being seen as an authority is a sure way to influence other people. Social Proof has to do with external validation such as testimonials, endorsements, and media recognition. The intent is to be perceived as an expert, someone who commands respect.

One thing about expert status is that no one is going to anoint you as an expert, or at least it's not very likely. Some of us may make a major finding that has the media flocking to you, but the rest of us are going to have to declare expert status for ourselves.

Of course this may feel uncomfortable, especially if we are taught not to promote ourselves. Remember, you need to stand out in a "sea of sameness," and gaining expert status through publishing, media appearances, and the like will help you rise above the others in your field. I am not recommending that you buy yourself onto the best seller lists or run an ad on a well-known website and then say "As Seen On" in your communications, as some advocate, but you have to stand out. You can have all the credibility in the world, but if no one knows about you, it won't matter. I remember something Scott Simon once said on National Public Radio in the US that is applicable here: "if you're talking but no one is listening, why bother?"

Principle 3. You need to continually up your mental game at each level of success. Overcoming attitudes and behaviors that hold you back is mandatory.

One of the biggest hindrances to our own success is how we think about ourselves. Some self-doubt and self-criticism is common to us all, and we need to overcome feelings of inadequacy if we are to put ourselves in the public eye. We need to get beyond the "I'm not (fill in the blank) enough" syndrome. "I'm not good enough." "I'm not worthy enough." "I'm not ready enough." "I'm not smart enough." "I'm not educated enough." "I'm not talented enough." "I'm not successful enough." You get the point. Inner demons and fears come in all shapes and sizes, and they manifest themselves in the form of procrastination, delay, fear of criticism, etc. One favorite phrase for this kind of thinking is "head trash." You need to engage in waste management or you won't be able to overcome your blocks.

In addition, we want to be comfortable, but if we are going

to stretch, we need to be uncomfortable. One coach is known for saying that if we are comfortable, then we should be concerned. Being uncomfortable is the new normal. Let's face it – growth requires that we reach beyond the familiar. No one ever achieved anything great by staying where they were.

Besides being uncomfortable, we need to reevaluate how we view the attitudes of others towards us. We want people to like us, but sometimes we have to be hard-nosed. We care about what others think of us, but if we care too much, we are going to try to please everyone. Daniel Amen, the **Change Your Brain, Change Your Life** author, once said that at age 18, we are so young and confident that we don't care what others think. At age 40, we have a reputation to protect, so we spend lots of time worrying about what others think. At age 70, we realize that no one has been thinking of us all along. This may be funny, but there is a big grain of truth here. One of the biggest obstacles I have seen is that we are paralyzed by worrying about what others think of us. We don't want to offend anyone, so we are willing to play it safe and not allow ourselves to appear foolish.

One person puts it this way: "Your opinion of me? None of my business." This attitude may be somewhat difficult to achieve, given our childhood conditioning to seek approval, but we can't go around with the fear of what others think. Don't make the mistake of thinking that you can go through life without stepping on someone's toes. I guarantee you that no matter how hard you try to be liked, there will always be someone who doesn't like you. It could be how you part your hair, the colour of your shirt, the way you hold your pen. People are triggered for all kinds of reasons, and you can't worry about it. The sooner you can free yourself from the need to be liked, the better.

It is worth noting that some successful personalities are deliberately obnoxious, and they gain a large following by insulting others. And, of course, they are not above poking fun at themselves. In the US, radio host Howard Stern constantly berates his guests as well as those in the public eye who somehow displease him. He has called another radio show host a "fat pumpkinhead," laughing at his own rudeness. His deliberate polarization of his audience – some love him, others hate him, but few are neutral – is a key to his massive success.

Not caring about what strangers think is one thing, but we also need to be on guard against the naysayers and critics in our own midst. For some people, their family can be a huge obstacle. Jealous parents often resent the success of their children and will sabotage their efforts. Siblings can also play the role of spoiler.

Principle 4. People buy for their reasons, not yours.

There is an old saying, "if all you have is a hammer, everything looks like a nail." This adage is related to the idea that people do things for their own reasons. I once knew someone who developed a technology that was far ahead of its time. He thought that everyone should see things his way, but they saw things their way. And they didn't want what he had, no matter how great it appeared to be. As a result, his company couldn't find buyers, and it folded. People buy what they want when they want. There will always be cases of outright manipulation, but in general people do what they want for their own reasons.

You can't force people to see things your way, no matter how much you would like. You can give people good incentives to buy sooner rather than later through techniques of influence and persuasion (guarantees, bonuses, sales, discounts, special offers, etc.) but people are a lot more wary than you might think when it comes to buying decisions. One of Cialdini's six principles of influence is Scarcity, and he shows how marketers can employ

Scarcity tactics to encourage action. A limited time offer is one such method, as everyone knows that the great deal will come to an end at a specific time. The clock is always ticking, and it can be an important way of influencing specific behavior.

Zig Ziglar said that everyone's radio station is the same. WIIFM or What's In It For Me. You can't get people to see things through your eyes. They will always see things through their eyes. If you can make the viewpoints match, then you have made progress.

Principle 5. People buy on emotion and justify on logic.

People may think that their decisions are rational, but scientists have found that people are highly emotional creatures driven in large part by forces they are unaware of. As a result, your communications are first processed by your prospect's emotions, which are found in the subconscious or unconscious. Our first reaction is the lower brain function of "fight or flight," not the higher brain "what is the return on investment of this choice?"

When we hear an unfamiliar voice shout "Hey You!" in a parking lot, we immediately look up without thinking. That is our lower brain at work. Our response is automatic, and there is no rational calculation involved. If we find that someone is warning us of an oncoming car, our reaction will be immediate and we will jump out of the way. If, on the other hand, we find that the person turns out to be an old friend who is simply saying hello, our reaction will be entirely different. In both cases, it is only after we have processed the information via the lower brain that we can let the higher brain take over and rationally assess the situation.

The following is the cover of the January 2014 issue of Scientific American. It shows a brain submerged in water, and the article says that our unconscious mind is basically running the show. We may like to think that our rational, thinking brain is in total control, but that's not true.

Scientific American, January 2014

When you speak with someone, you are first being received by their unconscious. If the "lizard brain" accepts you, it passes your message up to the conscious mind. (The process can take a millionth of a second.)

For marketers, this means that you need to make sure your message is accepted by the lower, emotional part of the brain before it can be rationally evaluated. Buyers are often swept up in emotions and make buying decisions based on them. If you remember **Trading Places** with Eddie Murphy and Dan Ackroyd, the buying frenzy in Orange Juice futures at the end of the movie occurs largely because other commodities traders have bought first. This "piling on" is very typical. Some marketers employ "fake shoppers" to initiate buying, hoping that others will follow their lead.

Principle 6. Stories are the best way into your prospect's mind.

The best way into the unconscious is through stories. You are much more likely to be liked and be given the attention you are seeking if you use stories to gain attention. If you want to win your way into your prospect's buying centre, the best way to do it is through stories that convey emotion. From early on, we learn through stories, and the "once upon a time" backdrop puts us at ease, far from the world of spreadsheets and facts. Recent studies have shown that stories are the most effective forms of communication if you want to be remembered.

Marketing legend Joe Sugarman, author of **Triggers** and other valuable books, recounts that practically all of his ads contain stories to draw the audience into his subject matter. "Just the facts" won't work nearly as well, as we seek a context that will make us feel on familiar ground. Sugarman is a master at telling stories during his speeches, and he reports that his stories are what his listeners remember, sometimes years later. As a result, he teaches through stories instead of simply presenting the facts. One person claims that stories are "data with a soul," and most of us respond better to stories than bare data.

One of the most important stories is the Hero's Journey, made famous by Joseph Campbell and Bill Moyers in the 1980's. Campbell found the Hero's Journey archetype in myths and cultures across time, and his research shows that this universal story has a profound hold on the human mind. In **Star Wars**, director George Lucas used the hero's journey as the foundation for his script. He consulted with Campbell to ensure that the story followed the traditional pattern of the hero myth. In its simplest form, this pattern is one of Hero-Obstacle-Treasure. The hero or heroine battles dark forces in order to win a treasure. The obstacle can be performing a heroic deed such as solving the Riddle of the Sphinx (Oedipus), overcoming a wicked stepmother (Cinderella), or defeating the enemy in battle (Achilles).

Today, you will see the hero's journey being recreated in a myriad of ways in commercials, advertisements, movies, novels, and even business stories. Each of us is a hero or heroine in our own story, and marketers who can help us become heroic will have a much easier time of winning our acceptance than those who try to sell based on facts and figures.

Principle 7. Promotion is one of the most valuable activities you can engage in.

Whether you like it or not, you need to engage in promotional activities in order to get the attention you want. For many of us, promotion means self-promotion, and this behavior can go against our upbringing. Some of us are taught not to self-promote, and such reluctance can be a stumbling block. According to the highly successful entrepreneur Meir Ezra, three of the seven divisions of a typical company should be engaged in some form of promotional activity, whether it is cultivating the press, advertising, marketing, or cultivating relationships in social media. Functions such as finance, product development, manufacturing, or human resources play a much smaller role in the success of the company. Let's put it another way: if you have something to sell but nobody knows about it, how successful can you be?

Principle 8. Business is very simple. Sales minus Cost equals Profit.

Bill Gates used to say that business is simple. You have Sales, you have Cost, and the rest is Profit. Now it's easier to make a lot of profit if you are a monopoly, but you get his point. One problem is that a lot of people over-complicate this simple equation. They confuse the three variables and end up going out of business. They don't look at their costs and consequently undercharge. They discount at the first sign of buyer resistance. They think of profit as evil and don't have any. And you've probably heard the amusing story of someone who sells products at a loss and says that they make it up on volume.

Getting back to Gates' simple description, you need to have sales if you are going to have a business. Sales can be thought of as the lifeblood of a business. It is what makes everything work. We will talk more about this vital function in a later chapter, but I need to point out here that if you are afraid of sales, then you need to change your attitude. Bringing cash in the door is vital to a revenue-generating company. You can have losses in the early days while you are developing your products, but lack of sales is the number one business killer. For most anyone reading this book, you need to grab sales by the hand and own it. If you aren't comfortable asking people to buy, you had better get comfortable.

Sales occur because the seller offers something that a buyer values and is willing to pay for. This is, I hope, entirely obvious, but you won't believe the number of companies who build products because they like them, only to find out much to their dismay and surprise that buyers don't care about them or won't pay the asking prices. You can't make the market want what it doesn't want, and don't ever forget that.

Costs can come in many forms, the most obvious being the cost of the product or service being sold. You sell a widget, and you know that it costs you a certain amount to make or buy one. So far, so good. One often overlooked cost is what it takes to acquire a customer. A few years ago, the inbound marketing company Hubspot calculated that it cost them $3000 to acquire a new customer. Now that's a lot of money by many standards, and not everyone has the business model to support it. I've seen many companies go under before they got off the ground because they couldn't get paying customers fast enough to offset all the other costs at work.

Let's talk about the concept of Lifetime Value of a Customer. All smart businesspeople know that they don't necessarily make a lot of money on the first sale. The only way that a company offering 12 books for the price of 1 can survive is by calculating that every customer who signs up will be worth a certain amount of money down the line. Cigarette companies find that smokers will spend about $150,000 on their products during their lifetime. (I'm not sure how ironic it is, but even a few people inside the tobacco industry admit that smoking cuts years off your life.)

Some companies intentionally lose money to bring in a customer, and this idea could take a little getting used to. Lose money to make money? The concepts of a loss leader or free sample come to mind here. You need to watch your metrics very carefully and account for all costs when you determine how much to charge. Some companies who offered discount coupons through organizations such as Groupon forgot to limit the number of discounts offered and ended up overcommitting. I heard about an oil change promotion that had the service station booked far beyond capacity, leaving many customers unhappy if not irate. If you take your eye off the ball, you could find yourself in a conundrum.

When you subtract Costs from Sales, you are left with Profit. To some of you, this word may trigger negative sentiments. Occasionally we hear about a Big Bad Corporation and its "obscene profits." Or we hear about a company being bailed out by taxpayers because of Losses, or Negative Profit. Whatever your opinion of Profit, it is worth noting that you need money to exist in this world. For businesses, Profit can fund new products, expansion, research and development, and any number of initiatives. You want this number to allow you to grow and also to give back.

We have a tendency to over-complicate things, and often we believe that the more complex, the better. But the opposite is true. We should strive for simplicity. You can tinker with the three main variables to your heart's content, but it all boils down to money coming in the door and money going out the door. If you don't get this equation right, you won't be in business very long. Every day you need to think about how to achieve your top line objective. Sales is the cure to a lot of business problems.

Principle 9. Doing the right things is more important than doing things right.

Jay Abraham, business expert, is quoted as saying that far too many entrepreneurs focus on the wrong things, wanting to get it right and not make mistakes. If you are not engaged in activities that advance your business, especially revenue-producing activities, it doesn't matter how few mistakes you make. I know lots of entrepreneurs who are afraid to go out and ask others to buy their product or service, so they hide behind their computer, so to speak. Yet hiding isn't going to lead to revenue. Examples of hiding include fixing your website, going through emails, surfing the web, and engaging in administrative tasks. Believe me; you need to focus on the activities that will pay off for you. If you don't want to do them yourself, you will have to delegate that responsibility to someone else.

Not all activities have the same value, and you need to manage your time so that you focus on high-outcome activities while leaving others undone or performed by someone else. You need to differentiate between high-payoff tasks and low-payoff tasks. Having products and services for sale will bring in revenue. Having a clear message will make your value proposition more understandable to your target market. Promotion and publicity will bring in buyers. Don't make the mistake of being busy with minor tasks and confusing such activity with real accomplishment. Some activities can be worth thousands of dollars per hour, whereas others will never be very valuable. Don't confuse activities with accomplishment.

Some examples of high-payoff activities include product development, meeting with prospects, and developing sales and marketing programs. Low-payoff activities are such mundane chores as buying groceries, doing yard work, and surfing the web with no specific purpose in mind. If you want to get ahead faster, you need to delegate the low-payoff activities to others or use your "less productive" time to take care of these tasks.

Principle 10. You need to take care of your health. If you don't have energy, stamina, and the ability to put in the hours required, you are in trouble.

The need to always be doing can have disastrous consequences on your health. Although doctors did not realize the effects of diet and exercise on one's well-being until fairly recently, you need to take care of yourself so that you have enough energy and powers of concentration to get the job done. Burnout affects all of us at one time or another, and you need to guard against it. Being busy is hardly an excuse for neglecting your health, but that's what I have found with many people. Coke and a candy bar is not a substitute for real food, and sooner or later this type of lifestyle will catch up with you. If you want to be there when it counts, you need to develop healthy habits and live according to them.

Principle 11. Know the Natural Rhythms of Your Body and Mind

Your body has natural cycles, and you cannot be at peak performance 24 hours straight. You need to look at your productivity according to the time of day and make adjustments so that you are not working contrary to what is natural for you. Some people get up at 4:30 AM and thrive on the solitude of the early morning. They find that they can be twice as productive before others get up or arrive at the office. On the other hand, others are late risers or take an hour to find their rhythm. Trying to get these people into an early morning routine simply isn't going to work. Each person has a natural bodily cycle and their own sleep requirements, and you need to find when you are the most productive. Your cycle may change with the seasons, and you need to adjust your waking and sleeping patterns with your work schedule. Don't fight Mother Nature, as they say.

Principle 12. Don't beat yourself up if you don't seem to be "getting everything done." There will always be more to do.

A lot of people suffer from being overwhelmed, and then they lament the fact that they didn't get everything done. Let me assure you that you will never get it all done. If you are growing personally and professionally, there will always be more to do. But this doesn't mean that you should be working all the time. You need your downtime, periods where you recharge your batteries and get out of the busywork. In fact, it is often when you are

"Get Your Message in Motion and Make Money" produced and presented by David Shiang, focuses on how to develop your personal story (the foundation of your business) and get it into the marketplace successfully. He has given multiple workshops to more than 600 people on this topic over the past year, and people loved them. One woman told him that the 3-step formula he introduced crystallized the story she has been trying to put together for the past decade. He goes into great depth on how you can apply his formula to your specific situation. We talk about YOU and YOUR MESSAGE and how you can multiply your effectiveness and profitability a hundred-fold. For a Free offer visit:
entrepreneursolutionsinc.com/GYMIM

About David Shiang

David Shiang is the President of Open Sesame Marketing & Communications, a consulting and coaching firm specializing in helping clients make quantum leaps in their businesses and personal lives. David is a graduate of MIT and has a Master of Management from the Kellogg School at Northwestern University. He was also a Danforth Fellow in the English PhD program at UC Berkeley. He has broad experience in marketing, strategy, coaching, consulting, research, and education.

not working that you are at your most creative. So when you are working, be focused, but leave time for relaxation and just letting it go.

In the next chapter, we're going to delve a little bit more into your mindset, which is what drives everything. As they say, "you become what you think about." You need to have a healthy mindset and attitude if you are to survive the inevitable obstacles that arise on the entrepreneurial journey.

Free Offers

- **Get Your Message in Motion and Make Money**
  "Get Your Message in Motion and Make Money" focuses on how to develop your personal story (the foundation of your business) and get it into the marketplace successfully. I have given multiple workshops to more than 600 people on this topic over the past year, and people loved them. One woman told me that the 3-step formula I introduced crystallized the story she has been trying to put together for the past decade. **For a Free Offer Visit entrepreneursolutionsinc.com/GYMIM**

- **Skyrocket Your Life with The Heroine's Journey**
  No matter where you are in life, you are on a journey. The Heroine's Journey, the feminine version of the Hero's Journey, is the most powerful archetype that helps us deal with our own life's ups and downs as well as the highs and lows of those we serve. You are the heroine of your own journey. The focus of the VIP Intensive is putting the Heroine's Journey to work in your life and business. If you

don't know how to use this archetype, which is an integral part of your DNA, you are at a disadvantage.

For a Free Offer Visit entrepreneursolutionsinc.com/SRYL

2. Mindset and Motivation

Out of the thousands of things
you can obsess about, only 3-4
matter right now.
–Perry Marshall

Developing the entrepreneurial mindset is one of the most important things you can do. When you are your own boss, when you can't go running to someone else for cover, you had better know why you have chosen your path in the first place. As they say, "Know Your Why." You may want freedom, unlimited income, a lifestyle business that allows you to be with your kids, or the ability to work from anywhere in the world. All of this is possible when you call the shots. And only you can tell yourself why you do what you do. When things don't quite go your way, you need to draw upon your "Why" for support and inspiration. You can't rely on the contradictory advice you are going to get from others.

In this chapter we're going to look at some of the less-talked-about characteristics that make up successful entrepreneurs. Some of them may go against your own nature, which is why you need to be fully aware of them.

You Can't Do it Alone

Giving up control is one of the hardest things for an entrepreneur to do. We are brought up to be self-reliant, and we think we can do it all. As a result, we can take on more than we should and find ourselves overwhelmed and confused.

There are tasks that we are good at and others that we are not so good at. As I mentioned earlier, experts say that each of us excels at about 5% of what it takes to succeed in business. We can get by for a while doing the other 95%, but sooner or later, you will need to delegate and share the work. You don't want to try to become an expert at 100% of what needs to be done, which is often our first inclination. No, you can't do it all.

Outsourcing is one way to get things done, and there are ways of finding people who are willing to work for a lot less than you might imagine. In the Philippines, you can find college graduates with excellent English skills who will work for $5 an hour. You can also take on partners or employees as you grow. The bottom line is that you have to recognize your limitations and take action accordingly.

Stop Doing Certain Activities

In addition to outsourcing some tasks or finding partners to take care of them, there are probably specific tasks that you should stop doing. Period.

We all know that there are many tasks and activities that

need to be done. What many of us don't realize is that others can be abandoned completely without consequence. You probably have many habits that take up time but produce no return. You may want to keep some of them, but you are probably unconscious of many of them and therefore don't know how much time you are wasting away.

I suggest that you keep a journal of all of your activities for a week or two. You will be amazed at how many things you are doing that actually don't contribute to the business. Some of these can be done by others, but some should not be done.

The concept of Open Loops is applicable here. Activities have a cycle: Start, Change, Stop. You initiate a task, something gets accomplished, and you come to an end. When you complete a cycle, another begins. The problem lies in too many open loops that are not closed in a timely fashion, if they are closed at all. Each Open Loop is like an item on your "to do" list, and anything still open stays on the list. If your "to do" list gets unwieldy, you are going to be overwhelmed. I am willing to bet that you have tasks from more than a year ago not yet done. Any Open Loop adds to your stress level. Reorganizing your files and the boxes in your attic may be an Open Loop. One solution might be to throw them out rather than sort through them meticulously. (Some de-clutter experts argue that other than "must save" information such as financial statements or personal information, you should throw out anything you haven't consulted in a year or two.) The existence of the Internet makes such a practice more workable, as much is available online that couldn't be found a few years ago.

Think of Open Loops as Unfinished Business that you should take care of as soon as you can. The longer these Open Loops stay open, the more your mind will be filled with "things I need to do." De-cluttering your mind will allow for clearer thinking and better decision-making. Your brain has a limited capacity to focus, and confusion is the enemy of clarity.

Watch How You Spend Your Time and Track the Results of Your Activities

Does this sound familiar? You spend all day running around and are crazy busy, and when the day ends, you wonder what you accomplished. "Where did the day go?" you ask yourself. If this happens to you on a frequent basis, you are likely the victim of being overwhelmed, poor planning, lack of focus, or all of the above. You are not lazy, it's just that there is so much to do that it's hard to work on one thing at a time. Use the 80/20 rule to help determine what to focus on. Also known as the Pareto Principle, it states that 80% of your results come from 20% of your activities. 80% of your sales comes from 20% of your customers. Pareto's Principle can be applied in a myriad of ways and can be drilled down to estimate that 1% of your customers will spend 50x the amount of your typical customer. Such estimates can be helpful with product planning and pricing. The principle is very powerful and can accelerate your success practically overnight.

In addition to looking at your activities carefully so that you focus on high-payoff ones, you need to measure results. One hour invested in crafting a marketing campaign is likely to bring in more sales than moving the boxes in your office. Yet I would be willing to bet that you have, on occasion, avoided working on high-payoff tasks for one reason or another. You need to focus on activities that bring in sales as one of the most important things you can do. If you don't want to engage in sales, you need to find a partner or alternative method to accomplish this all-important function.

Feed Your Mind and Develop Good Habits

Entrepreneurs should always be growing and developing themselves. If you aren't learning, you are being left behind. Despite what Ecclesiastes said about there being nothing new, there are always new developments that you should know about. Technological innovations never cease. New ways of automating and outsourcing can cut huge amounts of work down to small tasks. What used to take hours to analyze can be done in minutes due to new data analysis techniques. You should spend time each week, if not each day, in developing your skills and learning how to better yourself. As Ben Franklin said, "An investment in knowledge pays the best interest."

Break Free of the Need to Be Right

The need to be right affects all of us to some degree. Who wants to be wrong? Who wants to admit that they made a mistake? Yet this need is one of the most insidious habits we can have, because it damages relationships and can lead to arguments and behaviours with disastrous consequences.

The need to be right shows up in many ways, not just the need to have the last word in a conversation. By insisting that we are right, we keep ourselves in a zone of comfort and safety. Even if we are not particularly happy with our situation, being right allows us to remain the same. We do not have to change. (The only person who likes change is a baby with a wet diaper.)

Look at the figure below, which is a simplified version of Thurman Fleet's Stick Figure.

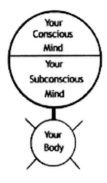

Thurman Fleet Stick Figure

I mentioned earlier that the brain filters information through the Unconscious first and then passes "acceptable" information to the Conscious Mind. The Unconscious Mind (or Subconscious Mind) doesn't want to change – it is perfectly happy with the way things are. Its first instinct is to repel anything new. We are "right" wherever we are at the present moment. Admitting we are "wrong" is uncomfortable and requires that we somehow change, somehow disturb our present state. When we feel challenged with new information or offered a way out of our circumstances, it is often easier to reject the new and stay put in the safety of where we are. The brain's need for safety and security is very strong and is one reason why it is so hard to change.

How many times have you said to yourself "they don't get it" when someone rejects change that could improve their situation? This is the Unconscious at work keeping the person right where they are. Tony Robbins once said that 85% of the people who attend his programs go home and do nothing. The interplay between the Unconscious and the Conscious Minds help explain why so many of us reject change. It is often easier to remain where we are than to enter into a new and unknown future, despite the positive changes that could result.

Seek Advisors and Coaches

Entrepreneurs are often Type A "take charge" personalities who love to blaze their own trails and do things their way. As a result of this trait that can be called "rugged individualism," they are often reluctant to ask for help or assistance. Even if they know that an investment in their own growth or education can pay off many times over, they may want to "do it all" rather than seek help (regardless of cost).

Those who seek fast progress should learn from someone who has already "been there, done that" rather than try to reinvent the wheel. Learning from and emulating successful role models can mean the difference between years of frustration on one hand or an accelerated journey on the other.

Finding people to advise and guide you is the other side of the coin of knowing that you can't do it all yourself. No star athlete would compete without having a mentor or coach, and the same is true of smart entrepreneurs. Mentors and coaches can come in many forms, from an informal support group to individual coaching. Having an advisory board to guide you would be wise, and hiring a business coach to help you improve in any number of capacities is typical of high performers who want to make expedited progress with as few bumps in the road as possible.

Think of Ways to Add Value to Others

I quoted Zig Ziglar earlier: "You can have everything in life you want, if you will just help enough other people get what they want." This statement contains a large element of truth. Think of ways that you can add value to the lives of others, and the rewards will come back to you. Scientists have recently found that being a caring animal could be part of our nature. Monkeys who were offered the opportunity to help other monkeys did so, foregoing food and other pleasures in the process. The scientists were surprised, as their model of animal behavior is based on selfishness and survival. They thought that the monkeys would abandon the others and that selfishness would rule. They were wrong.

What this means for us is that altruism has many beneficial aspects and that helping others can lead to an immense payoff. Business is a win-win proposition, and those who practice win-lose will not stay in business for very long. Businesses that succeed in the long run provide value in exchange for money or another form of compensation.

Know When to Move On

Although this book is about entrepreneurial success, I need to talk about failure. But before I do, let's remember what Winston Churchill said: "Success is not final, failure is not fatal: it is the courage to continue that counts."

Failure is something we are all used to. You didn't learn how to walk overnight. You didn't learn how to ride a bike on your first try. You fell down. And you got back up. It's the getting back up that is the key, not failing in the first place. Not everything goes according to plan. Do you remember the dot com bubble in the early 2000's, where company after company disappeared overnight and stock options that had seemed so valuable were suddenly worthless? Nothing was about to save these companies from failure. Yet the world didn't come to an end.

Sometimes you need to accept that an idea isn't going to work out as expected. If you can't adapt quickly enough, you may have to call it quits and start over. Fortunately for us, our economic system has a safety net for the smallest entrepreneur as well as the biggest corporations. One option is the bankruptcy code, which allows a company to fail and start over with a new slate. There used to be a saying, "What's good for General Motors is good for America." If that is true, then the 2009 GM bankruptcy, which allowed them to wipe out billions in debt, cancel contracts, and walk away from many of its obligations, was also good for America.

No one wants to consider the possibility of failure, but it does happen. The trick is to fail fast and learn the lessons that are there to be learned. Don't bleed a slow, painful death. Instead, accept reality and call it quits if there doesn't seem to be a viable alternative. The march of progress is going to run over some companies. They may be unable to compete due to poor management, or they may be in a market that has suddenly changed. Newspapers and magazines, once the undisputed king of media, have shrunk in size if they are still publishing at all. No one is really at fault – new technology completely disrupted their business.

3. Sales, Marketing, and Money

*To Nothing happens until
someone sells something.*
–Attributed to Thomas Watson,
Sr., founder of IBM

Everyone knows what sales is. Sales is what makes the cash register ring, although these days not everyone may know what a cash register is. Sales is revenue, the top line, ka-ching, money in the door, the act of buying, the transfer of money in exchange for a good or a service. The aim of a profit-driven business is to bring in sales that exceed the cost of fulfillment and delivery. As we saw, Profit is what is left over after you subtract Costs from Sales.

Defining marketing is a little trickier, and even at Fortune 100 companies, the role of marketing isn't always clear. Often sales takes the lead, and marketing plays a supporting or subordinate role. That is partly because sales is very easy to measure: either you have orders and cash coming in the door or you don't. But according to Peter Drucker, the father of modern management, marketing drives sales. He wrote the following a long time ago:

> "Because the purpose of business is to create a customer, the business enterprise has two–and only two–basic functions: marketing and innovation. Marketing and innovation produce results; all the rest are costs. Marketing is the distinguishing, unique function of the business."

A contemporary of Drucker's, marketing Professor Phil Kotler, said that the aim of marketing is to make selling unnecessary. Marketing encompasses an entire array of activities that are designed to makes sales easier. Promotion, publicity, advertising, pricing, positioning, branding, messaging, communications, and distribution are only a few aspects of marketing. One issue is that measuring the effect of such initiatives on sales is difficult at best for many companies, especially brick and mortar enterprises. Marketing initiatives are designed to work together, and sometimes you can't tell whether it was pricing, advertising, or store shelf position that caused customers to buy. John Wanamaker, owner of the first department store in Philadelphia, is famous for saying, "half the money I spend on advertising is wasted; the trouble is I don't know which half."

Online, it is easier to measure the effect of the elements of your "marketing mix," as testing is much more precise. You can run A/B split tests where half of your visitors see one offer and the other half sees another. If one pulls better than the other, then you will see if you can improve the higher performer and discard the lower performer. The line between Sales and Marketing has become increasingly unclear, partly because of the Internet. If you can buy from a company's website, is it due to Sales or Marketing or both? The answer may be academic, but there is no doubt that you need to focus on bringing in the money if you are to succeed in business.

Money brings with it a whole host of issues. Some of us are not well-prepared to receive money. Some of us are brought up with the idea that having money is bad or evil or that anyone who has a lot of money is dishonest. Such thinking can be a major obstacle on the way to success. Each of us needs to be sure that we are ready, able, and willing to accept money and success.

Pricing is another issue when it comes to money. I know many entrepreneurs who are afraid to raise their prices out of fear that their customers will go somewhere else. Or they themselves wouldn't pay premium prices, so they don't think others will either. We can't go deeply into pricing here, but price and value have a lot to do with each other. Figure out how to add more value to your offerings, and you can raise your prices. You can also include guarantees and other methods of reducing buyer resistance and perceived risk.

Business is About Psychology

Business is about making a sale, an exchange of goods and services for money. You have to know how to value your offering and make it so compelling that people will trade money in order to have it. No matter where you are positioned on the price spectrum, whether you are selling the equivalent of a utilitarian Chevrolet or a luxurious Cadillac, perceived value is key. Transactions and relationships are based on what goes on between people and how perceptions are shaped.

We've covered a bit about emotion and the need to engage people at an emotional, unconscious level. In order for an exchange to occur, there has to be an emotional transference so that the buyer desires what is being sold and is willing to trade money to obtain it. Transactions seldom occur in an emotional vacuum. People may want to think that they are driven by logic alone, but this myth is slowly being exploded. In **Predictably Irrational,** Dan Ariely has written extensively about our tendency to do things that seem rational to us but are irrational from an external perspective. Of more importance, he shows how businesspeople can tap our irrational tendencies to influence buying behavior.

Free Offer

To discover Five Secrets – Why you Need to Market to the Unconscious Mind and How to do it Successfully
For a Free Offer Visit entrepreneursolutionsinc.com/MTTU

Messaging and Your Unique Selling Proposition (USP)

Why should someone do business with you? That is a question that you must be able to answer at the drop of a pin. One problem I have seen repeatedly over the years is that the messaging of a lot of businesses is muddled, confusing, and complicated. And as they say, "the confused mind doesn't buy."

Other key questions that you need to be able to answer include:

- Who is your target market?
- What is their big problem or big pain?
- What it your solution?
- How is it different?
- Why are you worth what you are charging?

- Why should I buy from you instead of your competitor?
- What kind of guarantee do you offer?
- How much risk am I taking when I do business with you?

Far too many entrepreneurs have garbled messages, or they sound very much like everyone else. I hear entrepreneurs talk about their business and I don't know what they offer and why it is of value to the buyer. They have trouble differentiating themselves from others, and as a result they are put in the category of the "sea of sameness."

If you don't have a clear Unique Selling Proposition (USP) or Unique Value Proposition (UVP), you need to develop one quickly. You need to stand out and have a clear reason why your ideal client would want to do business with you. You don't have to say that you are better – in technology, having better features is often transitory – but you have to show how you are different. And the differences better be ones that your customers value.

Your uniqueness can come in many forms, even in businesses such as nuts and bolts. Just make sure through testing and real world experience that your difference is along a dimension that your market cares about. I have seen numerous companies try to be different in a way that has no value to buyers. If you are touting speed of delivery but the market does not place a value on this attribute, you need to differentiate in another way. Here are some ways you can differentiate yourself from the competition:

Consistency – McDonald's may not have the best hamburgers, but people know what they can expect from the chain anywhere they go. This level of familiarity goes a long way towards making it safe and predictable for customers to eat there.

Customer Experience – you can offer customers an experience they won't find anywhere else. Disney theme parks are one example of a unique experience.

Delivery – you can offer guaranteed overnight delivery or some other characteristic that sets you apart. Domino Pizza built its business by guaranteeing hot pizza within 30 minutes.

Guarantee – you can offer a unique guarantee. Today, money back is almost a necessity at retail stores. Some such as Zappos added free return shipping.

Pricing – you can guarantee that you will match competitors' prices, as does Best Buy.

Product – you can have a unique product, such as Bose radios.

Quality – you can cite premium quality products or services. Rolls Royce, for example, offers the highest quality at high prices.

Service – you can cite superior customer service. Nordstrom has long been known for exceptional customer service, and it charges premium prices to offer such a high level of service.

Value – Whether you are offering high prices or low prices, people want value. The restaurant chain Denny's chain offers a great value for budget-minded patrons, whereas Ruth's Chris Steak House offers excellent value at the high end. No one would ever mistake the two chains, yet they each offer their own definition of value.

Traffic and Conversion

In the online world, Traffic and Conversion are two of the most important words you will hear. They are used offline, of course, but given the ability to track every click a prospect makes on their computer, they take on new meaning in the online world.

Simply put, your website needs Traffic. You need to take your Traffic and Convert it to Leads and then to Buyers. If you can do that effectively, you can have a business. There are now billions of web pages, so getting Traffic has never been more competitive. There are a myriad of ways to attract visitors, but two of the most important are SEO (Search Engine Optimization) and Paid Advertising. Regarding SEO, if your website has the right keywords and content, a person might come across it through searching on one of the search engines such as Google or Bing. With Paid Advertising, you typically pay when someone clicks on your ad. Depending on the platform you choose, you may be able to have your ad seen by millions without charge; it is only when someone actually clicks on your specific ad that you end up spending money.

Google Adwords was one of the first large-scale pay per click (PPC) vehicles. Many businesses had little idea of how it worked, causing them to throw money down the drain due to what one person called a "Stupidity Tax." On the other hand, Adwords allowed small weavers in the middle of New Mexico to sell blankets around the world, something that could never have been done before. Companies selling the Internet riches dream told every Tom, Dick and Heidi that they could run a business from anywhere in the world with just a computer and an Internet connection. There is a bit of truth to this, of course, but making it work isn't exactly as easy as one might believe.

Making SEO and Paid Advertising work has become a massive industry. There are now thousands of companies specializing in all aspects of making business perform on the Internet. Optimization has become part of our vocabulary. But keep in mind what I said earlier about the FUD Factor. You may recall that FUD stands for Fear, Uncertainty, and Doubt. One dirty little secret of the technology industry is that it thrives on instilling FUD in the minds of users. There is a lot of mumbo jumbo and double-speak in technology, some of it put there intentionally to confuse people into buying. Now this is not to say that FUD is always used to manipulate us. Technology can be very confusing, and just keeping up is a daunting task even for professionals in the industry. And there are certainty plenty of honest technology providers out there. But there are also some where "buyer beware" is the watchword. And let's face it, if you have a problem, you are often going to spend money to solve it if you can't do it yourself. How many of us can go very long without our computer? (Maybe it's not a coincidence that the illegal drug industry and the computer industry are the only ones where the customers are called "users." Technology is an area where "don't try this at home" is almost a given for most of us.

Visibility and Credibility

You've probably heard the acronym AIDA, which stands for Attention, Interest, Desire, Action. In order for someone to take the action of wanting to do business with you, they need to know about you first. In other words, you need to get their attention. You need visibility.

In today's market, getting visibility is one of the biggest problems facing the entrepreneur. There are billions of web pages. There are probably hundreds if not thousands of companies that do something similar to what you do. And while the concept of visibility is simple, many entrepreneurs have a fear of visibility. They really don't want to be seen, they don't want to be vulnerable. This can be a huge obstacle to success.

Credibility comes with fulfilling expectations, being

dependable, and doing what you say you will do. There is a lot more to credibility than just serving the customer, but that is a big part of the equation. It helps if you have credentials and an impressive track record, but all too often people with fancy resumes don't get the job done. Woody Allen is quoted as saying that "80% of success is showing up," and it helps to have testimonials, a solid background, top-tier schooling, and great references. The good thing is that even people without the above can still succeed if they implement just a small fraction of what I am sharing in this book. If you are just starting out, you can gain credibility over time. No matter where you are in your business, credibility can and does work wonders. But it won't matter if you don't have visibility.

One of the best and most important ways you can gain visibility and credibility is to write and publish a book. Authors have always held an elevated place in the minds of others. When you tell people that you wrote a book, they often have a higher opinion of you than they would otherwise. Many people use books as calling cards, and Kindle has become a lead generation vehicle for savvy entrepreneurs.

Speaking in front of groups is another way of obtaining visibility and credibility. Blogging, using press releases, networking, sponsoring your event or someone else's, and using Social Media (YouTube, Facebook, LinkedIn, Twitter) are other ways of gaining visibility and credibility. Each of the above can involve specific strategies too complex to cover here, but the bottom line is that if people don't know about you, they can't do business with you.

The Need for Honesty

Why did marketing guru Seth Godin write a book called **All**

Marketers Are Liars? That's the real title, but he changed it slightly after people got the wrong idea. (Or was it the right idea?)

Here is a bit of background. Godin's book was published with the title **All Marketers Are Liars**. Not surprisingly, there was a bit of a backlash, as some wondered whether this was giving marketers a bad name. For his revised title, he added the words **Tell Stories** and crossed out **Are Liars**. Shown below is the "new and improved" title.

The funny thing is that Godin didn't change a single word of the actual contents of the book. All he did was give it a different title. One might ask, are the stories that these marketers tell called "tall tales"?

Have you ever heard of the terms "sleazy salesperson," "used car salesperson," "hustler," "bait and switch," "pushy," "annoying," or any other negative description when describing sales and salespeople? We are trained to be on guard when someone is trying to sell us something, no matter how good their product or service may be for us. When Godin used the term "Are Liars," he meant that marketers have at their disposal an array of influence and persuasion techniques that can induce people into buying. Because some people are easily persuaded, there are consumer protection laws designed to ensure that people who may get swept up in their emotions have a "cooling off" period during which they can change their minds.

As an entrepreneur, you need to guard against using hype and manipulation, and you should offer a solid guarantee. If you take advantage of people, it will come back to haunt you. As they say, "what goes around comes around." Keeping your word is one of the most valuable ways you can instill confidence and trust in buyers and prospects. Without confidence and trust, you can't last very long in business.

I remember the case of someone who pitched a fairly expensive seminar to a roomful of people, and he promised to reveal his secrets to those who bought. He told everyone that he wouldn't give the seminar unless all of them came. Yet he gave the seminar despite the fact that one-third of the room didn't purchase. He broke his promise, plain and simple. I'm sure he had his reasons, but several people who heard about the matter refuse to buy anything from him ever again. He lost their trust. And once he did that, it is very hard to gain it back.

Match Your Offering with Market Desires

You've probably heard the old adage, "Find a need and fill it." While this saying contains an element of truth, people don't buy what they *need*. They buy what they *want*. A lot of people need to lose weight and exercise, but how many actually do it? And why people buy isn't as simple as you might think. The psychology of what makes someone desire one thing and not another can be very complex.

In addition to bringing out offerings that match market wants and needs, you have to listen to the market and learn from it. While relying on what the market tells you for new products can be tricky, you can observe the market in action by studying consumer behavior. The market will tell you about price points, product requirements, and a host of other key issues. If you are not in touch with your prospects and customers, you are missing a key ingredient for success.

Grow Through Partnering, Referrals and Affiliates

Few companies can grow significantly on their own. Direct sales to buyers will always have a place, but today a company can call upon an array of methods to broaden their reach without having to invest in significant internal resources. Distribution channels such as retail networks, affiliates, sales partners, and other partners are available. The Internet allows a company to go global with a fraction of the investment required only a few years ago.

Smart companies, especially service-based ones, will have referral strategies in place. Someone offering financial planning services has natural partners such as accountants and lawyers. By seeking win-win strategies, a company can be introduced to strangers via a trusted partner and thereby gain trust much faster than they would be able to build it on their own. Word of mouth is still one of the most effective forms of advertising and is a key strategy for many companies, especially network marketing companies. And one of the main driving forces behind the growth of social media is its ability to spread the word quickly to people all over the world.

4. **Shortcuts and Resources**

*Give me six hours to chop down a
tree and I will spend the first four
sharpening the axe.*
−ABRAHAM LINCOLN

This chapter showcases specific tools, technologies, and websites
you can use to accelerate your success. You need to constantly
be on the lookout for anything that can help you automate,
streamline, outsource, simplify, and go faster. Why do things the
hard way if you don't have to? Why engage in low-level, low-
payoff tasks when you can find others to do those for you while
you add value elsewhere? Keep in mind that due to the fast-
changing nature of business, not all of these tools and technologies
shown below may work exactly as I've described when you read
this.

Everyone knows about Google, Facebook, Twitter, Pinterest,

and LinkedIn, so I'm not going to go into detail about them here. Instead, I want to let you know about some lesser known websites, tools, and techniques that can make a huge difference in accelerating your productivity. In some cases, you can accomplish in minutes what used to take hours. I am also mentioning little-known uses of some well-known sites that will help you research trends, competitors, and the like.

Before I list some great resources for you, I want to tell you a story I heard about the importance of knowing shortcuts. I know someone who had central air conditioning installed six years ago. The technician told the homeowner to turn the air handler on manually whenever the thermostat was set to "Cool" so that air would circulate all the time. This required a separate trip to the basement, as the air handler was located a floor below the thermostat. The homeowner had noticed from the beginning that whenever the thermostat was set to "Cool," the air handler turned on automatically. However, he did what the technician told him to do, which was to go to the basement whenever the air conditioning was turned on and manually turn on the air handler. Curious as to why he was doing what he was doing, the homeowner finally called the air handler manufacturer and asked about the manual switch on the machine. He was told that there was a setting on the thermostat that would allow him to turn on the air handler so that it would run continuously. As a result, a trip to the basement was not needed. The homeowner had been given incomplete information at the start and had been making unnecessary trips up and down the stairs for six years! Knowing one shortcut will save him time and energy in the future. I am sure that there are many shortcuts you don't know about. I know that I learn about them all the time, and they are a key factor in allowing me to do more with less.

Selected Shortcuts (in alphabetical order)

Amazon – use book titles, descriptions, and reviews for copywriting purposes. You can discover words and phrases that resonate with your target audiences by looking at various books.

Creativelive.com – a site that offers free and paid classes by experts on a variety of subjects.

Curationsoft.com – a site that helps you find content from all over the web that you can curate for your audience.

Elance – a global talent source where you can find suppliers and also find business.

Fiverr – a global talent source where you can find suppliers and also find business.

Googlekeywordtool.com – information on SEO, keyword ranking, analytics, and much more. (Not affiliated with Google.)

Guru.com – a global talent source where you can find suppliers and also find business.

Hubpages.com – a community site to collect and share information, especially for authors.

Kindle – can be used to scope out the competition, whether for books or topics. For authors, a valuable method of generating leads.

Nozbe.com – an online tool that helps you organize time and projects.

Pingmyblog.com – distribute your blogs automatically and increase your visibility and credibility.

WriteMonkey.com – provides a user interface free of distractions so that you can better concentrate on the task at hand.

Yasiv.com – shows visual relationships between Amazon books and other Amazon offerings. This can be handy for research purposes and competitive analysis.

Selected Resources (in alphabetical order)

80/20 Sales and Marketing,
by Perry Marshall

Getting Everything You Can Out Of All You've Got,
by Jay Abraham

Influence: the Psychology of Persuasion,
by Robert Cialdini

Instant Income,
by Janet Switzer

Predictably Irrational,
by Dan Ariely

No B.S. Wealth Attraction for Entrepreneurs,
by Dan Kennedy

Websites You Should Know About

Free Press Release Distribution
http://mashable.com/2007/10/19/press-releases/

Insights for Entrepreneurs
http://www.forentrepreneurs.com/sales-marketing-machine/

Outsourcing to the Philippines
http://youwillneverworkagain.com/outsourcing_mastery/

Organize Your Social Media
www.tweetdeck.com
www.hootsuite.com

Sitemap Generator for Google Rankings
http://www.freesitemapgenerator.com/

About the Author

Rick McCulloch is the CEO of Entrepreneur Solutions, a division of G-Logic Solutions. He is also a Founding Member of NEURS, a global organization dedicated to helping entrepreneurs succeed. McCulloch's specialty is helping entrepreneurs "Do More with Less" in today's constantly-shifting business environment. He accelerates growth and expedites success by strategically connecting the dots, uncovering underutilized assets, leveraging overlooked opportunities, and finding hidden resources that allow businesses to prosper. By providing insight and clarity, he helps entrepreneurs de-FUD (decrease the Fear, Uncertainty, and Doubt that so many feel in today's crazy, fast-paced world).

Entrepreneur Solutions empowers dedicated entrepreneurs to accelerate their success by giving them the tools they need to work *on* their business so that they can be smarter when working *in* their business.

With insights gained from over twenty five years of industry experience, we are well qualified to help clarify what it takes for the entrepreneur to get in front of those who matter to their business, break through to their customers' needs and help identify areas of the business where the entrepreneur needs to focus their efforts to be more successful.

We also collaborate with a wide variety of specialists in marketing, accounting, finance, corporate structuring, and information technology to provide additional value.

We serve new or existing entrepreneurs who have a strong commitment to their business, well-defined goals, and marketable customer solutions. In addition to our affiliation with NEURS, we have ties with the Association of Petroleum Engineers

Geoscientists of Alberta, Canadian Society of Petroleum Geologists, American Association of Professional Geologists, Calgary Chamber of Commerce, and leaders in energy, technology, and business.

A Special Offer for My Readers

Entrepreneur Solutions offers a complimentary **30 Minute Small Business Assessment** that will give you and your business more focus, clarity, and control. Here is what we accomplish together in this fast-paced, no-nonsense telephone session:

1. Gain an understanding of your goals and what is holding you back from achieving them.
2. Pinpoint the specific roadblocks in your business that you must remove in order to increase your odds of success.
3. Identify ways to accelerate your progress – now and going forward – by revealing little-known shortcuts, tips, and techniques that apply to your specific situation.

By the end of the free call, you will have greater clarity and insight into your business. You will know specific action steps you must take if you want to succeed. Guaranteed.

The **30 Minute Small Business Assessment** is conducted personally by me, Rick McCulloch, not by a member of my team. Please be assured that this is not a thinly-disguised sales presentation. I will give you my best insights based on more than 25 years of industry experience and a lifetime of learning. There is no charge, but the value to you could well be priceless.

The assessment will typically take place within 1-2 weeks of your request, based on availability. There are a limited number of available openings. To secure a slot, call me at 1-403-910-0311 or email rickm@entrepreneursolutionsinc.com. I will advise you regarding availability and will provide you with a pre-consultation questionnaire that allows both of us to get maximum value from the consultation.

Visit my website entrepreneursolutionsinc.com for insights, resources, and additional information.

CPSIA information can be obtained at www.ICGtesting.com
Printed in the USA
LVOW11s1433050415

433236LV00008B/48/P